A Glimpse of Grace

* * *

"Grace has been dead for 20 years . . . . Yet, when I make changes outside or inside my home, or in my life, I still ask myself: What would Grace think . . . what would Grace do?"

> —*Marian Salt*
> Spokane, Washington and Tucson, Arizona

"She had more sense and energy than any of us."

> —*Bill Bell*
> New York City and Arlington, Virginia, remembering Grace's impact on Bill and his friends, all in their 20s, after World War II.

"But for Grace Jones, there never would have been a restored Campbell House."

> —*Helen Enloe*
> Spokane, Washington

* * *

GRACE, AGE 20, IN HER FIRST STUDIO

A Glimpse of Grace

by M.G. Bassett

Published by Ulyssian Publications, an imprint of Pine Orchard, Inc.
Visit us on the internet at www.pineorchard.com

Printed in Canada.

9   8   7   6   5   4   3   2   1

ISBN 1-930580-27-4

Library of Congress Control Number: 2001097333

Dedicated to the Memory of
POLLY D. JONES

. . . who early sensed
her daughter Grace
lived to create
and to share
beauty.

APPRECIATION

For calligraphy, design, and text production, I am grateful to graphic designer Jeanne McMenemy. Liz Hall, Connecticut artist, added valued layout advice.

Northwest photographer Hans Matschukat took and selected pictures of people and places. Institutions, too, were generous.

The Northwest Museum of Art and Culture, courtesy of curator Marcia Rooney, gave shots of the Campbell House. This historic mansion was Grace's last passion.

Yale University led me to churches her father built.

The Spokane Public Library uncovered pictures from the first to the last of her life.

Whitman College offered reproductions of two men in Grace's life: Joe Bassett and David Gaiser.

The pristine Newman Lake Peninsula was caught by the camera of Chris deForest, director of the Inland Northwest Land Trust.

I am indebted to the artistic members of the Aldworth family, owners of the lake cabin built for Grace, for pictures of her lake and town homes. The Aldworths are Bill and Ann; their daughter, Susan; son, Craig; and grandson, Spencer Brown.

I thank the Parsons School of Design for a picture of Frank Alvah Parsons, from whom Grace learned in New York. In Spokane, designer Bill Farrington learned from Grace. His widow, Marcella, graciously contributed a picture of her husband.

ACKNOWLEDGEMENTS

First, I thank Sandy Worley, who reproduced this text repeatedly. Next, I am grateful to three journalists:

- Jean White of *The Washington Post*;
- Dorothy Powers of *The Spokesman-Review*;
- Fran Lewine of the Associated Press and CNN.

I am uniquely indebted for editing volunteered by Barbara Blakemore, my Columbia University classmate, executive editor of McCall's, editor and fiction editor of other national magazines in New York; to Jean Porter, lawyer and newspaperwoman, whose contributions of ideas and time could come only from an old friend; to Helen Ward Myers, law office manager and organizational genius; and to Fred Richardson, international businessman, and his wife Mary, retired to Spokane.

For guiding me to historical accuracy, I am grateful to journalist Nancy Coleman from Neath, Pennsylvania; to Nancy Compau, historian at the Spokane Public Library; to Craig Aldworth, Spokane engineer and history buff; and to the Dayton Historical Depot and, among its patrons, Darlene Broughton, Faye Rainwater, and Mary Jacob. Founding of Congregational churches in Ritzville, Medical Lake, and Spokane was recollected by clergy and members.

Finally, I thank my artist cousins Constance Bassett and David Cann of Stockton, New Jersey; and Elizabeth Harris and Hans Matschukat of Walla Walla, Washington. All are able, like Grace, to convey beauty seldom seen.

A Glimpse of Grace

CONTENTS

Prologue

Grace Jones was born in January 1891 at Neath, Pennsylvania. She died in December 1981 at Spokane, Washington. Her 90-year life was a search for beauty. It began with drawing, painting, making designs. It developed into a half-century career as an interior decorator. When others joined her in her search, it gave her great joy and energized her into a companion to be treasured. She lived with a zest, wit, love, and understanding that still kindle warm memories among those who shared her company.

"Grace has been dead for 20 years," said Marian Salt, one of a family of Grace's friends for three generations. "Yet, when I make changes outside or inside my home, or in my life, I still ask myself: What would Grace think . . . what would Grace do?"

Her impact on me, her niece, is unforgettable. I write this biography because I want to show how a woman, responding to a century of enormous change, can enrich lives.

To begin, after Grace died, I went to her birthplace: Neath. You won't find it on a map. West of New York City; south of Binghamton, New York; northwest of Philadelphia. I asked my way along. At a country store on a cross roads to which I had been directed, an old man came from the back room and said: "Of course, I know where Neath is. Just up this road." He pointed. "To a white wooden sign on the right. Says 'Neath.' Turn left."

After I turned left, trees opened to a ledge and beneath, spread a vale transplanted from Wales. A church with a picturesque spire, a graveyard, pastures, a few houses, and a stream trickling beyond. This was the beautiful, independent little vale Grace could not remember.

She was a baby when her Welsh father and English mother carried her West, where she lived most of her life and died. I stopped on that hilltop and could only say to myself, "How fitting. How blended the green of the valley, private, lovely, yet strong." I felt her presence and that of those who introduced her to this country.

Her roots were British; their origin, Celtic. Grace's father, John David Jones, left Wales to study for the ministry at Yale. When he was graduated in 1885, his fiancée Polly Davies left her family, her friends, and her country to marry him. They settled in Pennsylvania.

Together, studious John and lively Polly nurtured their three children—Clifford; Olive; and the youngest, Grace—in Victorian values. Grace's response was to live by strict standards herself but to develop tolerance toward the moral, religious, and ethical values of others.

In 1891, the family moved west to Washington state. It was a time when great fortunes were being made and lost. But the Jones family, indifferent to money, focused on the spiritual. They moved from town to town, where John organized congregations and churches. By the time Grace was 15, she had attended four different schools.

Grace turned to her mother, more than to her father, for comfort in childhood. Polly Jones gave an easel to Grace, aged three. Her mother encouraged opportunities for Grace to express herself, in contrast to the more stern advice of her father to befriend the friendless, to work for the church, and never to complain. Grace, at age 15 in 1906, experienced a momentous turning point in her life. She wintered with her mother on Southern California beaches near Capistrano. What they shared focused her young artistic development.

The decade between 1908 and 1918 prepared America for maturity. It was a directional decade for Grace as well. Americans, by confronting the death and dislocation of the First World War, began to see the need for a new inter-nationalism and a more fair society.

Grace's life offers a parallel. Her great loss was the death of both parents. Her father died in the spring of 1907, when Grace was 16, a high school junior. Dr. Jones contracted pneumonia from a chill while he was plodding through deep snow on Spokane's South Hill, searching out a new church site. Grace's mother died suddenly in 1914 of a burst appendix. Grace was 23. These two blows propelled her out of her parents' world into her own. She broke away to New York and Europe, training her artistic talents and absorbing other cultures. Thus prepared, at age 30, she knew herself and where she was going.

In the high-flying '20s, Grace was dead serious about starting an interior decorating business. Declining offers in

New York, Kansas City, San Francisco, and Houston, she returned to Spokane, where friends and former painting students formed the nucleus of a clientele.

It was a time when most women her age reared children, made their homes their lives, and might have experimented with bathtub gin and smoking for the first time. Grace made herself a part of the families of those women who became her clients, enriching their lives and environment by beauty and expanding their appreciation of design.

Each decade of her half-century career impacted her life and work. In the Great Depression of the 1930s, when most people had little or no money, Grace prospered. She collected fees from those who could pay and carried on her books those who could not.

During the Second World War, Grace decorated rest and rehabilitation centers for the military in the Philippines and Hawaii. She could not go into the war zone, so she collected room and window measurements, ordered fabrics, had chairs upholstered and curtains sewn, and shipped them off to furnish rest centers for soldiers, sailors, and Marines. After the war, she expanded her buying trips to San Francisco and the Orient while still making her annual visits to New York and Chicago.

In the 1950s and '60s, Grace revitalized her work by reaching out to both the past and the future. She immersed herself in the restoration of the historic turn-of-the-19th-century Campbell House in Spokane and increased her contacts with college students, decorating sorority and fraternity houses throughout the Pacific Northwest.

Her decorating career spanned nearly 60 years from 1920 to the mid-1970s. Then, in her 80s, Grace's eyesight dimmed. She lost her trusted assistant with the death of Clarence Heineman, who worked at her side from age 18 to 83.

Grace Jones lived before the era of dot-com. She worked and thrived in an environment that today's business woman is hard put even to imagine. She never went to an international conference of business women. Who would have attended in 1920? Women had barely received the right to vote. She liked to play golf. But her chances to practice were limited. Almost all golf courses were reserved for men. Social clubs barred her because she was single.

She was too busy for resentment. Nor was it in her character. She never campaigned to change society.

Instead, she followed her star, developed her talent, and shared her perception of beauty as the Grand Design.

CHAPTER ONE
Childhood

THE GRADUATE, 1909

Churches of her childhood

Neath, Pennsylvania

Medical Lake, Washington

Dayton, Washington

Childhood

G race did not remember the little vale in Pennsylvania where she was born in 1891. Nor are there any official records of her birth. The courthouse burned down. So, for many of the people born or buried before 1895, in this replica of the hillsides and vales of her father's native Wales, it is almost as though they had not lived. But not for Grace.

It was January 7. The midwives had left footprints in the snow that blanketed the hill between the white church and the Victorian house atop the slope above. Grace was born easily, the third and last in her family, and the tiniest at six-and-a-half pounds.

GRACE'S BIRTHPLACE

Grace was less than a year old when her family boarded a train for the West Coast; else she would surely have remembered Neath, the transplanted Welsh hamlet.

Her father John David Jones, a native of Gwenagle in Wales, had just earned a Doctorate of Divinity degree

DR. JOHN D. JONES

from Yale. As she had promised four years earlier on a beach in Southern England, his fianceé Polly Davies left her family, her friends, and her country to cross the Atlantic to marry him. They were reunited in an era of high ideals, sensitive to human frailties, symbolized by Grover Cleveland, one of the nation's strongest Presidents. A Presbyterian minister's son, Cleveland, when he went to the White House shortly before Polly and her young minister John were married, was trailed by taunts about his rumored fathering and abandonment of an illegitimate child. The jingle echoed throughout the last of the 19th Century:

Ma, ma, where's my pa?

Gone to the White House.

Ha, ha, ha.

Like many European immigrants flooding into the country at this time, they left personal foibles behind for an idealistic try in the New World. The young couple chose to live among friends and families from the old country for a while. Their choice was Neath, Pennsylvania, settled in the 1820s and 1830s by Welsh from Glamorgenshire. The newlyweds, John and Polly, traveled from New Haven by way of New York City to be briefed on Neath by John's immediate predecessor at the Neath Congregational Church, Dr. E. J. Morris.

The Morrises fed them a familiar Welsh dinner, meat and potatoes and sickam, a jellied oats served with milk. Dr. Morris, at that time, minister of New York's 11th Street Welsh Congregational Church, briefed the couple on the 50 some worshippers awaiting them in Neath: oldsters clinging to sermons in the native Welsh language; their need for organization of the church women; and the church as the center of the area's social life. Then the young minister and his wife set out by train so far as it ran, and the rest of the way by horse-drawn coach. When John and his lively lady Polly arrived, the minister at the reins, one can imagine the welcoming dinner in the parish house, the short organ solo, and prayer.

The scene remains. The lane on the wooded hill opens on the vale below, the church tower at the center of fewer than 10 houses, a few fenced barnyards, and the stream leading out of the vale. In between the Pennsylvania Dutch to the south and

FIRST CHURCH OF GRACE'S FATHER

the New York Dutch to the north, the names in the graveyard beside the church are Williams, Thomas, Jenkins, Jones, Morris, Davies, Roberts, Owen, Griffiths, Upham—none but Welsh names.

John was between 26 and 31 years of age during his Neath ministry. He left, unfortunately, no sermons. One clear contribution was that he substituted English for Welsh in his Congregational church. By the time he left, in 1891, the only services in Welsh were held once a month in private homes. Polly organized a ladies' aid society her first year in Neath and guided the churchwomen in sewing and entertaining at the church. The women formed a book club as well and discussed writings that far exceeded strict religious bounds. Their collection formed the basis of a large library maintained in the church to this day.

Grace's older brother and sister, Clifford and Olive, remember family picnics at a clearing on the treed banks of the valley stream. Their father and mother discussed his sermons, and he rehearsed them in between games and toe dipping in the water.

The young minister took his family West to Washington state in 1891, continuing his life's work, building Congregational churches, organizing congregations, and moving on to other towns to build and organize more. Until Grace was two, she lived in Ritzville from 1891 to 1893; from ages three to nine, in Medical Lake between 1894 and 1900; from ages nine to 15, in Dayton between 1900 and 1906. These are all small towns in Eastern Washington.

When she was 15, the family moved again to Spokane and chaos followed for Grace. She was torn from the first deep friendships she had formed in Dayton. Her older brother and sister were off to college, leaving her to bear the full burden of helping her parents start church and home life all over again. Grace dreaded starting again for the fifth time. She knew nobody. Equally unknown were her well-educated and genteel parents. Her new high school was a two-mile walk for her. She could not bear the changes and collapsed a few days after she enrolled. That led to four months in Southern California with her mother Polly and a reinvigoration of Grace, preparing her for new crises to come.

The Joneses were in and out of Ritzville in two years. Flushed with his successful weaning of his Pennsylvania congregation from Welsh to English services, Dr. Jones met more determined loyalty to their culture and language from German immigrants in the Ritzville area. They came from the Volga and Black Sea, driven there in part by religious schisms in their native Germany. Some worshipped at Dr. Jones' First Congregational Church despite his sermons in English. The congregation split twice, first to the Zion Congregational Church and then to the Philadelphia Congregational Church. They worshipped in German for years after Dr. Jones left his tiny English-speaking church, which was torn down by its own congregation in the 1920s.

When Grace was a toddler in Medical Lake, her father saw as many people inside as outside of the state institution for the insane near his church. As a small child, she saw little difference between people inside and outside the bars. For instance, one inmate was instructed by her father for a First Communion. When the day came, her father, proud of the patient's progress, passed the cup and said, "Drink ye all of this, for this is the Blood of our Savior Jesus Christ...." The man gulped down all the wine, exhausting the church's supply. After sufficient time had passed to cool the hysteria of the moment, Dr. Jones asked the man why.

"You told me to," said the surprised supplicant. "You said to drink all of it."

Grace remembered the contented hours she sat with her mother on the steps from the street leading to the lake on the town's edge. She worked at the easel her mother had given her. They watched the sun's pattern on the water and, daubing colors from her paint kit, Grace created patterns of her own. At tea time, she learned how to hold her cup, to welcome guests, to talk with the ill-at-ease. "I never made friends at parties," she recalled, "because my father told me to talk to the children who had no friends." Perhaps her only childhood friends were a brother and sister, Raymond and Myrtle Enloe. Both remained close to Grace for the rest of her life. Years later, Myrtle said to Grace, "Your mother was the first lady I ever met." She made friends with horses. She drew them. They were to her beautiful, so graceful, and she wanted to move with them. Occasionally, when her parents put her in the saddle, she could not stop laughing with delight from the time the horse started until he stopped.

At nine, Grace was uprooted for the third time. Her life became more complex, more pleasant, and more tied to her community. In 1900, the family moved to Dayton, Washington, at the urging of Dr. Stephen B.L. Penrose, president of Whitman College. Penrose, a fellow Yale man, had built a congregation in Dayton from fewer than a dozen people. He wanted Dr. Jones to build the church.

Dayton, near the Lewis and Clark Trail at the intersection of the Snake and Columbia Rivers, drew many of the first Northwest pioneers. The town was bigger than Seattle in the 1870s. Families of some of these early settlers were in their second and third generations. So, Grace's new friendships extended beyond the church. She had stimulation in school. She went to slumber parties with the Broughton girls, who came from a large first family and lived in a towering house with a wrap-around porch, fronting on a block-long stone wall. Another family, the Peabody's, originally from Massachusetts, took in the Joneses, too. Mr. Peabody published the local newspaper. His only daughter Ernestine, along with the Broughton girls, were the closest friends of Grace and her big sister, Olive.

Grace also was exposed to stimulating adult conversations. Dr. Penrose, Yale 1881, formed what was known as the "Yale Band," initially a group of Yale Divinity School graduates and later expanded to include all Yale men who made the Northwest their home. They met in each other's homes each year. When they gathered at the Jones' house, after a few bars of "Boola Boola," they discussed for hours the spiritual, political, and social future of the Pacific Coast as they, at the turn of the 20th Century, foresaw it. Grace sat in a corner, listening fascinated.

Her father completed and dedicated the new Dayton church in July 1903. A high vaulted ceiling soared over the interior. There were two reception rooms on the first floor with a kitchen in between. In the "fireplace room," the congregation gathered for coffee hour after services. Community clubs and civic groups held dinner meetings and receptions in the larger reception areas adjoining, and still do to this day.

Grace watched nervously as he raised money for its stained glass windows. This was a signal, since Dr. Jones never left a church until he had installed at least one stained glass window. When his family saw that window, they began to pack. It meant they would be off looking for a new church site in another place. And this time, the year was 1906 and the place was Spokane.

The last thing Grace wanted was to start all over again. Unlike her father, whose life's work was starting all over again— another congregation, another church, another community— she had found friends, good teachers, time for her painting, and a rich Western history in Dayton.

Yet, on June 7, right after her sister's graduation from high school, the inevitable began. The family gathered with members of the Dayton church to announce Dr. Jones' new association with the Corbin Park Congregational Church in Spokane. Corbin Park had no church buildings, only temporary quarters for a few people who dreamed of a new church. Across town,

Dedication in 1903 of the Dayton, Washington, Congregational Church

the established Westminster Congregational Church had urged Dr. Jones to lead its congregation.

"Westminster does not need me," Dr. Jones told his family. "Corbin Park needs me."

Grace dared not ask the provoking question in her mind: "Does Corbin Park need him or does he need Corbin Park?"

Had she asked, her father might well have rethought his determination to build something from nothing and averted the chaos and death that was to follow in the next year.

With both her brother and sister at Whitman College, Grace faced alone the onerous duties of ministers' children. As she was starting all over again in a new town, allotting no time for her art, walking miles each day to a big school where she knew nobody, Grace collapsed.

"I'm so sick," she told her mother.

Polly Jones, her intuition as usual on target, immediately withdrew Grace from school and entrained for Southern

SWALLOWS OVER CAPISTRANO

California, where the two spent four months at Capistrano, the mission to which the swallows return.

She promised her husband they would return by Christmas. His work was to prepare a new home and church. Her work was to make sure her sensitive younger daughter recovered her health and her way.

By day, mother and daughter walked miles on the beach and rested in beach chairs. Her mother taught Grace the fundamentals of French. They did mathematical puzzles. They read to each other. And, Grace drew. With colored pencils, crayons and pastels, she created versions of her favorite place, where the sea and sky meet in ever changing patterns of sunset.

In the evenings, they played songs on the piano and sang in harmony. Their talks often returned to how Grace could continue doing, when she was grown up, what she had liked best to do in childhood and her teens. If art were to be her life, how could she earn a living? Would she have to depend on somebody else to give her money and time to continue? Or, could she combine art and life somehow, on her own?

Polly Jones told Grace about a man named Frank Alvah Parsons in New York City. He was making a successful living as an interior designer. And he was distinguishing himself by applying his artistry to both beauty and functionalism in home and office environments. He was about to join the faculty of the New York School of Art, which was to bear his name and share his talents for much of the 20th Century. Maybe, mother and daughter decided, they should keep an eye on

Frank Alvah Parsons to see what he could offer Grace after she finished high school and, if she chose, college.

Polly encouraged Grace to be her own person. With this support, Grace chose a new name for herself symbolizing her independence. It was "Consuela." It came from Spanish influences to which she was exposed for the first time at Capistrano: from Spanish music, which she loved, and from Spanish designs she was beginning to imitate. For the teenager, beginning to find herself, the name Grace Consuela Jones had a dignity and a ring she liked and, for the next ten years, she proudly wrote and spoke her name not as plain Grace Jones, but Grace Consuela.

One day, sitting by the Pacific, Grace asked her mother, "Will I draw when I grow up? Will I paint? Is that idle? Or selfish? What would God say?"

Her mother laughed. "Let's see if we can hear."

The ocean moved edges of the sand. Little whitecaps beat an irregular rhythm. The sun broke through the fog and seemed to be creating the sky beyond the horizon.

"There is a kind of beauty," said her mother, suddenly very serious. "Like a Grand Design. You are luckier than most other children. You hold that kind of beauty in your head. If you keep searching for it, you can re-create it and help others understand that Grand Design."

"Then, God wouldn't mind?" Grace asked.

"He will bless you, my precious Grace."

When Grace remembered that California morning, she said she always felt the sun and sky lighting a path for her toward color, design, and harmony.

Just before Christmas and Grace's 16th birthday, mother and daughter returned to Spokane. Grace was cured. She could not wait to do what she had previously dreaded—study at a new school, help her mother at home and her father in a church.

Christmas, 1906, was a happy time. The family reunited at their new home, 433 Cleveland. Dr. Jones presided over the midnight service at their temporary church in the middle of the block, bounded by Monroe and Virginia, later Grace Street.

Dr. Jones had a new idea. Sensitized, perhaps by Grace, to the division the Spokane River cut between the north and south sides of Spokane, Dr. Jones visualized bringing together the two sides of town. He noted that the major north-south thoroughfare, Lincoln Street, provided access to a potential church site from Corbin Park across the river, up to the base of the steep South Hill. Such a church could also draw as well from the affluent Browne's Addition to the west. So, he reasoned, a large community church could serve both north and south on the west side of town for the first time.

On a late night search for his idealized church site, Dr. Jones caught a chill. Yet, he returned the second cold night, trudging through snow. The chill turned to pneumonia. On April 7, 1907, Grace's father was dead.

His dream of a community church uniting the north and south sides of Spokane died with him. Instead a stone-block Corbin Park Church, substituted for his alternate site, was dedicated in 1909, two years after his death. This was on the corner of Lincoln and Cleveland, catty-corner from the Methodist church, now a community center, and a block from an Episcopal church.

Robert Hyslop, a lifelong Corbin Park resident, remembered, at 93, that the Congregational church was a childhood haunt. The rail to the front steps was smooth rock. On top, the surface rolled up and then down, and leveled off near the grass. "We children would ride our bicycles over on weekdays when the front door was locked. We would push each other from the top, down a wonderful roller coaster ride, to the ground."

Such childhood rides may have been the most lasting memories of this church. It was torn down by its congregation in 1923. Nor did the other two Protestant churches survive in this predominately Catholic neighborhood.

Grace was convinced that if fate had allowed her father more than his 11 short months of life in Spokane, his alternative church, formed only in his mind, still would be serving North, South and West Spokane today.

Grace was 16 when her father died. Her childhood was over.

CHAPTER TWO

The Young Woman

HER MENTOR

FRANK ALVAH PARSONS
PARSONS SCHOOL OF DESIGN
NEW YORK CITY

MICHELANGELO   RENOIR   DA VINCI

The Young Woman

At 18, how could Grace have imagined that a decade later she would plan and conduct a tour of European art capitals? Before she was 30, she had experienced:

- the loss of both her parents, each death strengthening her independence in very different ways;

- the study of music and art at Whitman College, which motivated her to explore deeply the harmony she sensed in both;

- her own art studio where china-painting lessons burgeoned into a thriving business;

- graduation from Parson's School of Design in New York City, fulfilling a childhood dream to make art and design her life, not just a hobby;

- a grand European tour, planned and led by Grace at the behest of an art patron impressed years earlier by Grace's painting lessons in Spokane;

the welcome home to a little chalet on the point of a heart-shaped lake near the Washington-Idaho border, a 60-year-long retreat for Grace, her "happy house."

One had to look sharply to catch a glimpse of this young Grace Jones. She darted, quickly and quietly. She was tiny, stretching to stand five feet tall. Her weight played around 100 pounds. Her cheekbones were high; her sapphire-blue eyes were deep set. Her chin was pointed, her nose aquiline. She was well proportioned.

Her most unusual quality was her enormous energy. She seemed to do more in a day than anyone else. Along the way, her wit, independence, tolerance, and tireless search for color won her friends and admirers, especially at Parsons, the first school for interior designers in the country.

She had to have drawn strength from her mother's example. Widowed at 47, Polly Jones faced, for the first time, the need to earn a living. When she asked her late husband's church about repayment of a loan of considerable family capital lent to the church, she was told the church considered that a gift. Polly did not dispute. "If that is what you wish, that is what shall be," she told the church fathers.

On the first Sunday after her husband died, mother and daughter set out for church. "Mother," said Grace, "you are going in the wrong direction." Polly replied, "From this day forward, I shall go to my church." Her church was Spokane's nearest image of the Church of England, the Episcopal Church. Grace experienced that Sunday the standing, sitting, and kneeling sequence of the Episcopal service with her mother. Afterwards on the walk home, her mother advised Grace, "There are many religions in the world, many churches, many ways to gain spiritual strength, which will enable you to be fulfilled and to help others as well." She told Grace she would have to choose her own way on the basis of her own experience and study.

Grace pondered that advice through the years.

More immediately communicable was her mother's verve. Once, when they were climbing Spokane's steep South Hill, the mother told her daughter, "I feel just like skipping up the street."

Polly Jones chose to work in real estate, one of the few professions open peripherally to women. Grace could help a little because her mother began to buy and sell houses and apartment houses, remodeling and renovating them before the turnovers. But Polly told Grace firmly that her first job was to learn and to finish high school. Through the summer, Grace and her mother and Grace's older siblings lived and worked together: Clifford in a bank; Olive in a greenhouse; and Grace, at her mother's side, in property negotiations and renovation.

Grace was enrolled in the classic courses at the forerunner of Lewis and Clark High School. She was graduated in 1908, with the highest grades among students taking these college preparatory classes. So it was Grace who became the serious student: not her big sister Olive who used to study Greek and Latin with her father; nor Clifford, the only son, favored in the British tradition of the Joneses; but little Grace, the paint dauber, she of the tart tongue, the dreamer. Her father would have been proud and, even more, surprised. Her mother always expected her to excel.

By this time, Grace had moved with her mother into a new home on Seventh Avenue on the brink of the South Hill. Polly now owned three rental houses, an apartment house, and a wheat farm. Precariously advancing her real estate career on credit, the new breadwinner was offered help by her oldest children, now incoming college seniors. Clifford and Olive suggested they withdraw from school to contribute to the family income. Their mother would have none of that. Instead, Polly moved to join her son and daughter at Whitman College in Walla Walla. She took Grace with her. Polly rented the property in Spokane and, with Grace, moved into a house just off the campus. There, the mother and her three offspring lived together for the last time.

Grace, aged 18 and 19, attended Whitman Conservatory. She had a sweet singing voice and never sang, except in harmony. Her ear heard a blend of sound, just as her eye saw a blend in color. She was more acute than introspective. So, she did not dwell on the "why" of this unity, only on its beauty. She could be found most often beside one of the streams that meander through the Whitman campus, at her easel, experimenting with the various forms, lights, and shadows of the water. She would concentrate on her canvas and her concept. Then, she liked to remain by the brook and think of the future. She knew she had much to learn to develop what she now recognized as a natural artistic talent. By now, she knew too, that

Grace, top left; her brother Clifford; and sister Olive lived with their mother as a family for the last time in 1910, near the Whitman College campus.

Frank Alvah Parsons was running that school of design her mother had mentioned to her those four long years ago at Capistrano.

In June of 1910, Clifford and Olive Jones were graduated. He went into banking, business, and marriage. She began to teach Latin and French in high school. Grace and her mother moved back to Spokane, back into the big house on Seventh Avenue, back to art for Grace and to real estate for her mother.

Grace, despite her artistic priorities, wanted to help her mother. Her mother was her best friend. But Polly Jones was wiser. She cautioned Grace to listen to her own drummer and never to abandon her art, if Grace truly believed that was to be her life.

Polly did allow Grace to help renovate and redecorate rental units for resale. This exercise was closely enough related to Grace's design ambitions to be, Polly believed, mutually advantageous.

Thus, mother and daughter supplemented each other's efforts until 1914. Grace was 23. Without warning, at 54, Polly died of a burst appendix.

Though devastated, Grace by then had absorbed enough of her mother's strength to withstand the loss. She continued to give her painting classes and, perhaps to help fill the void in her life, made two new friends, older women about the age of her mother.

The first was Maude Sutton, an original homesteader of nearby Newman Lake. Maude was an artist herself. Grace soon discovered that this new china-painting student had much to

MAUDE SUTTON

teach her about intricate design. Maude also showed Grace the lake's peninsula point, soon to become a favorite retreat for Grace and her friends. Giant, flat, volcanic rock slabs interspersed with evergreens formed the bluff, high above the water. There, one of Grace's friends, a schoolmate, Clarence Heineman, would sit for hours with Grace and Maude talking about Grace's ambition to have a home at the lake some day. Together, they visualized her cabin. And they planned together a cabin, answering such questions as: Would Grace like to see the sunrise or sunset from the terrace? Which would she prefer—the sun's warmth in the morning or in the evening?

Being single, how should she arrange sleeping quarters? How could they make sure kitchen odors didn't enter the living room? She would like to sit facing west, Grace said. She loved sunsets. She envisioned a wide wooden balcony with carved rails. Why not design a windway in between the cooking and living areas, so that lake breezes would waft to a rock terrace behind the cabin during the heat of the afternoon? And that would solve the location of the bedrooms as well. Men guests could sleep upstairs on one side of the windway; women, on the other. They congratulated themselves on their dream cabin, which Maude said she wanted to be Grace's "happy house." Clarence said he'd like to build it.

The second of these two older students was a wealthy matron, so impressed with Grace's love and talent for art, that she insisted that Grace, sometime in the next five or ten years, lead her on a European tour of art capitals.

With these and her other painting students, Grace busied herself to ease the pain of her mother's absence. She helped her brother and sister sell the Seventh Avenue house, turn over an apartment house, and rent the remaining houses their mother had acquired. They signed a long-term lease with a tenant for their wheat farm.

This enabled Grace to realize the ambition she and her mother had envisioned for so many years. She was off to New York to broaden her horizons and to study at the Parsons School of Design.

She arrived by train in the early spring of 1916. She was 25 years old. She treated herself to a hansom, liking horses more than the noisy new autos. Placing her two small trunks beside her on the double seat, she first saw New York from this horse-drawn carriage. They clomped across Fifth Avenue to 141 East Sixty-third, the address of what was then the Barbizon Hotel for Women. This was a proper and protected place for a young woman from another part of the country or living away from her family for the first time. For their safety, guests were checked out and checked in, and there was a curfew.

Once moved in, she headed for Fifth Avenue, which was to become her favorite haunt. She loved to see the display windows, to analyze them, and to redecorate them in her mind.

And the Parsons School of Design was even better than she had imagined. Particularly, she loved to extrapolate the color charts with oils, watercolors, and pastels into designs on her easel.

"Mr. Parsons," as she always called him, sometimes would look over her shoulder or sit beside her and work variations into his own design.

Parsons also conducted tours for students to see his own work in the mansions of New York's upper East Side, the estates along the Hudson, Winterthur, and other Dupont homes in Wilmington, Delaware. Grace never missed one of these trips.

To supplement her savings, she designed Christmas cards for Hallmark, a recently established Kansas City enterprise. The company hired Parsons' students to work from New York. Within a year, Grace went from being a low-paid part-timer to an employee so valuable that Joyce Hall, the company founder, urged her to join the firm after her graduation.

She had two other offers from fellow students to start a business together, one in Houston and the other in San Francisco.

Grace declined them all, choosing to return to Spokane. No more "starting over again" for her after five moves in the first 15 years of her life. She would tend her roots in Spokane, where her painting students and the families of mining and farm wealth could form a nucleus of a new and, she believed, potentially large interior decorating clientele.

But first, she had promises to keep. Her old painting student, the Spokane matron with a yearning for European travel, had been in touch. In response, Grace spent July and August, 1919, in New York, planning their long awaited art tour. By September, Grace was ready to advise her old friend on where to go, how long to stay, and what to see.

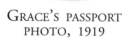

GRACE'S PASSPORT
PHOTO, 1919

They set off together, taking the Southern Atlantic route past Gibraltar into the Mediterranean. The trip, at first by sea, formed two large loops. In the Mediterranean area, this wound around Italy, Egypt, and Greece. The second loop encompassed France, the Alpine region, Holland and the Flemish country, and finally, England.

They lingered longest in Naples in southern Italy, Florence in the north, and in Paris and London. In Naples, Grace painted the sun rising and setting over the bay. She presented the oils to her patroness and a watercolor to her sister Olive.

It was a fantastic tour. And when they stepped off the boat in New York City, Grace was ready to concentrate on a career, her natural talents trained, disciplined, and educated not only by the grand tour, but by the first, and probably the best, school of design in the world.

After Christmas in Spokane, she spent January and February preparing to open her decorating studio in the early spring.

One Saturday in late March, Maude Sutton, the Newman Lake homesteader, and Clarence Heineman, whose sole ambition since age 18 seemed to have been to assist Grace in whatever she did, suggested they go to the lake. Grace agreed. When their horses stopped at the peak of the peninsula, Grace noticed a brown structure downhill to the west.

THE CABIN

She moved quickly down the hill to investigate, Maude and Clarence smiling on either side. There it was: the chalet, with the broad porch with hand-cut rails, the windway, the terrace behind, the separate sleeping quarters upstairs, and a native stone fireplace in the living room. Light streamed in from the gigantic glass-paned window facing west.

Maude and Clarence had built it while Grace was in New York: her chalet on the lake, her "happy house." Later, as they watched the sunset from the terrace, Grace knew she had made the right decision in coming home to Spokane. She was not to abandon her studio, her business, or her cabin for the rest of her life.

GRACE PRESERVED THIS PENINSULA POINT AT NEWMAN LAKE. NOW IT WILL BE PRESERVED IN PERPETUITY BY THE INLAND NORTHWEST LAND TRUST.

CHAPTER THREE

The Men in Her Life

GRACE AND CLARENCE

CHILDHOOD FRIENDS . . .

RAYMOND ENLOE

JOSEPH ELLIOT BASSETT

DAVID GAISER

LOYAL THROUGH LIFE

The Men in Her Life

G race was happily unattached.

She had two loves. One was art. The other was friendship.

Yet there were many men in her life: professional associates, admired artisans, husbands and sons in the families of her clients, boys young enough to be her sons whom she called her "troops" after their return from World War II, three childhood friends who remained close through their lives, and one man whose extraordinary 65-year-long attachment made him her trusted assistant and supportive friend.

In her professional life as an interior decorator, Grace met workmen whose skills she respected and salesmen who represented the great fabric and furniture houses of New York and Chicago. She entertained these traveling men at dinner or the theater, and sometimes offered a few refreshing hours of respite at her studio or lakefront cabin. From 1920 to the mid-1940s, Grace was the only decorator they visited west of the Mississippi and north of San Francisco. Then there were the men in her client families, sometimes spanning four generations, who often became good friends and welcomed her into their homes and social circles.

Grace also had her "troops." In their early 20s at mid-century, they were also friends of mine. As her niece, I was adopted by this band of World War II vets: Warren Raymond, Bill Bell, Dick Yancy, Bob Drumheller, John Heath, and Bob Southwood. We all were passing through Spokane on the way to the rest of our lives.

"Grace was our mentor and delightful companion," remembers Bill Bell, whose business, political, and government career took him to the Far East and, in retirement, back to New York. "She had more sense and energy than any of us."

On my 22nd birthday, Grace told me she would like us to spend a quiet day together at the lake. I had planned to celebrate with my circle of young friends but, of course, did not refuse the request of my favorite 57-year-old aunt. While I was swimming alone in the lake, Grace watched from a favorite perch on the giant Council Bluff at the peninsula point. Suddenly Bill, Warren, Bob, and Dick came running down the bluff, dived into the water, and swam to join me for one of the best birthdays of my life. It was a gift of friendship, typical of Grace. She understood others' deep desires. And she often set out, with the spice of surprise, to fulfill them.

But what of the men who affected her life deeply?

Clarence Heineman, who worked at Grace's side for more than six decades, was 15 when he first met her. Grace was 18, a senior at what became Lewis and Clark High School, demure, quick-witted, moving as though she knew where she was going.

He was a sophomore, awkward and unsure of himself. Clarence lingered on the outer circle of her friends, occasionally asking her questions. She was kind but distant.

When she opened her china-painting studio, Clarence, by then 18, asked her for a job.

"I can't afford to pay an employee," Grace said.

That was all right with Clarence. He would work for nothing until he could be a help, and then she could think about paying him. He could lift crates, deliver, pack and unpack china, fire the kiln, answer the phone.

Through the next three years, Clarence's confidence steadily grew. One of Grace's students, an older woman, often invited the two to Newman Lake. They sat on a rock ledge above Council Bluff, the point chosen by Indians to hold their councils. There, the trio talked about whether she would prefer to face the sunrise or the sunset when she finally built her own cabin.

Then, at 24, Grace began to envision a career as a professional interior decorator. Her mother had died a year earlier, and Grace was prepared to go to New York City to attend the Parsons School of Design. When he saw her off on the train to New York, Clarence sensed her electric excitement and must have had little hope of resuming their association.

Yet he could not let go. While Grace was away, he translated her mind's image of her lakefront cabin into reality. He built the cabin to face the sunset as they had discussed during their chats on Council Bluff. It was not a finished structure. But the cabin incorporated the two features Grace had treasured most—a windway separating the two sections and the carved wooden rails of a Swiss chalet.

Clarence was 26 when Grace returned from New York. He was a short man with straight black hair and black eyes. If he had no educated talents, he could offer loyalty, hard work, and devotion. These qualities were more than enough for Grace. By now, she sensed the capacity of Clarence to learn. He was a keen observer. So they opened her studio together. She was 29 and the year, 1920. It was the same arrangement as earlier. Clarence would help without pay at first and then, as income began to build, he would receive a percentage of the net.

Clarence freed Grace from the burdens of practical duties. He locked and unlocked the doors and drove Grace— sometimes long distances—to clients scattered throughout the Northwest. Over time, he became much more than a rug cleaner and carpet layer as he developed a sense of proportion, balance, and color. In the last 15 years of his life, he made buying trips to San Francisco, the Far East, and the Furniture Mart in Chicago. Grace saved New York, her favorite city, for herself.

Clarence continued to love the lake. When an evergreen fell, he planted a replacement. He built a wall of natural rock to support the cabin terrace. He lifted boulders from the shoreline or hauled them in a small boat from more distant points near the lake. This primarily non-functional but decorative stone wall was known as the "Heineman Memorial Wall."

And they shared many unforgettable moments. Once, Grace was reading in the living room when Clarence burst in, slammed the door shut, and began stacking furniture against it.

"Clarence, what are you doing?" Grace asked.

"Bear. Bear outside!" Clarence shouted.

"Don't be ridiculous," snapped Grace. "No bears come here."

She flung back the furniture and stepped out on the windway. Barely 20 feet from her stood a big brown bear, hungry, but probably more startled than she.

Grace flew back into the living room and frantically, with Clarence, stacked cupboards, chairs, sofas, and tables against the lockless and fragile French door. They sat, backs to the door, Grace visibly trembling. The bear padded onto the windway. Preferring the smell of the kitchen, he pawed open the door opposite, knocked a few jars off the kitchen shelves, and then, disappointed, lumbered up the hill and away. One does not forget experiences shared with a wild bear.

As Clarence became less robust in his 70s, bent almost double from increasing back sprain, he spent weeks alone at the lake. Grace would visit in the daytime, declining to stay overnight at the cabin. It was, after all, not proper.

One morning, Clarence, who had use of Grace's car when he drove to his home in the city from work at night, was late arriving at the studio. Two hours later, a concerned Grace took a taxi to Clarence's home. There was no answer to her knock at the front door. Then she heard cries for help. She went to the side window of a house that she never in her life had entered.

She saw Clarence lying crumpled on the sofa. "My legs. I can't move," Clarence pointed. Grace called an ambulance. There was a double break in one of Clarence's legs and a single break in the other.

Doctors ordered a blood transfusion for Clarence. Yet his condition did not improve. One night, Grace visited him longer than usual, staying until 8 p.m. As she was leaving, Clarence called her back to his bedside.

He lifted his right arm, placed his hand on the back of her tiny head, and pulled her toward him. Then, for the first and last time in his life, he kissed her on the lips.

"You'll be all right," she said, patting his cheek. She left immediately.

Three hours later, Clarence, at age 83, was dead.

"Why wasn't I kinder?" Grace asked when she told me this story. "You know, in all our lifetimes, I never touched Clarence until that night."

She had made, for her, a stunning discovery at Clarence's home. There were photographs of her on his desk, on his dresser, and on the walls. There were photos of the two of them together, at work, on trips, at social functions.

"Why didn't I understand? Why wasn't I kinder?" Grace asked again.

If Grace, as a young girl, ever imagined whom she might marry someday, the man probably would have been Joe Bassett, Raymond Enloe, or David Gaiser—the three childhood friends who remained close companions throughout the rest of their lives. Grace met each of them before her mid-teens. She knew their parents and families. They shared friends, common values, and similar educations.

Of the three, Joseph Elliott Bassett was the closest to Grace. Yet he probably would have been the most difficult for her to marry. She expected life to be hard and prepared for that. He wanted to laugh, to love and to live life fully, and was disappointed when he could not. How this handsome, funny, athletic, lover of nature appealed to Grace was, at first, through their mutual humor and, at the end, by their respect for each other's independence.

Joe was three years older than Grace. They met in their teens through their fathers, both Yale men and members of the "Yale Band," that little group of ministers, later expanded to include any Yale graduate who settled in the Northwest. When these men came to the Joneses, Grace from her seat in the corner never missed a word of what they said. At the Bassetts, Joe stayed outside to play tennis or baseball.

Joe's father J. D. Bassett had come West from Connecticut after Joe's mother Julia Selden had died. Between 1895 and 1900, J.D. established a "Bassett chain" of banks along the basin of the Columbia, a river he mistakenly envisioned as the future major transportation route for products and produce to the Pacific coast.

Soon the trains and trucks eclipsed the river's flow of commerce, and J.D. scrutinized more diligently the land and people of the great Columbia Basin for different investment opportunities.

GRACE'S CLIENTS AND FRIENDS OFTEN SPANNED GENERATIONS. OF MEN IN FOUR GENERATIONS OF THE AUTHOR'S FAMILY, SHE HAD THIS TO SAY:

JOHN DOWD (J.D.) BASSETT,
1857–1937
"That dear man."

JOSEPH E. BASSETT,
1888–1938
*"He spent the apex
and nadir of his life
with me."*

JOSEPH ELLIOT BASSETT, JR.,
1924–1972
"I lost him looking for him."

JOSEPH ELLIOT BASSETT, III
1954–
*"A very nice man…perhaps
most important."*

GRACE'S FRIENDSHIP WITH THE SHIELDS MEN
SPANNED THREE GENERATIONS.

GEORGE W. SHIELDS
Grace's Contemporary

JUDGE GEORGE T. SHIELDS
The Author's Contemporary

ANDREW SHIELDS
The Youngest Generation

His new idea was advanced for his era. He would found a new town. He chose a site, now Sacajawea State Park, on the south banks of the juncture of the Snake and Columbia Rivers, extending south to the Walla Walla River, a place where Lewis and Clark lingered in the first decade of the 1800s. J.D.'s town "Attalia" went up, rimmed by the three rivers and fruit orchards to the east and west. He built one of the first, and very nearly the last, privately financed dams in the West on the Walla Walla River. Its reservoir irrigated the orchards. In 1910, the dam broke and with it, the Bassett chain of banks collapsed. Attalia washed away. One of J.D.'s partners took bankruptcy; the other committed suicide.

Joe's father was State Senator, widely discussed as the next candidate for the U.S. Senate and a trustee of Whitman College. But his political, educational, and civic leadership was abandoned in J.D.'s concentration on working his way out of debt with the help of his suddenly serious son Joe. For the last 20 years of his life, he was state banking examiner.

Through all these crises, J.D. always was to Grace "that dear man." And Joe always could make her laugh or be serious through their first fumbling efforts to grow up. Joe, in his mid-20s, helped Grace, her sister, and her brother settle their mother's estate. This was time-consuming and somewhat intricate because Polly Jones had died unexpectedly, without a will. When Grace, in 1916, set out for New York, Joe told her to watch for him. He would come through, he said, on the way to "over there" to help fight "the war to end wars."

He did arrive in New York, but after the First World War was over. So Grace next saw Joe in 1919 when he was 31 and she was 28. He returned late because, after the Armistice, he remained for nearly a year in France with more than several trips to Paris, on a lieutenant's pay, without being attached to any units. Orders came for the units, not for Joe, to come home.

When his boat load of returning young officers docked, Grace was at the pier to welcome him home. It was a joyous and affectionate reunion.

"Joe was on top of the world," Grace remembered, "brimming over with plans for our homecoming celebration together in New York and with savings to re-establish himself in the Northwest."

Grace told me years later that Joe had shared with her both the apex and nadir of his life.

"I always have been grateful for that," she added.

The high point, she thought, was the ten unforgettable days he spent with her in New York that June. It was a celebration, not only for the war's end, but also of the cash and capacity he now had for the first time, to build a career and provide for a family.

Neither could have imagined that his low point was a mere dozen years away. In 1931, when Grace was 40 and Joe was 43, his bank would go under in the Great Depression.

In New York, Grace and Joe dined out every night. They went dancing. Joe took Grace horseback riding in Central Park and to a baseball game. Grace took him to art shows. They took in museums, plays, and an opera. Sometimes they simply walked, hand in hand, in different parts of the city.

They talked of their "can do" world of the 1920s. And they told each other of their ambitions. Grace would work in design to create beauty; Joe would work in banking and finance.

Since they both liked the water, they took boat rides around Manhattan and several times rode the fabled ferry to Staten Island. Whenever the ferry passed Ellis Island, Grace thought of her mother. When Polly debarked on that island from England, she yearned only to reach New Haven, Connecticut, and her Yale graduate to marry and raise a family with him.

As they stood by the rail of the ferry, Grace looked up at Joe and wondered how a woman could be so sure of a man as her mother was of her father. She was not sure at all.

Joe took a train for the West the next day. As he waved from his open window, Grace waved back from the platform. She knew instinctively that this, in important ways, was a final good-bye. The pleasure Joe had packed into those 10 days in New York, even the prospect of marriage and children, could not match the fulfillment she felt when her creativity was released by her diligent application to the principles of color and design. She knew nobody else, only she herself, could provide for that.

One more time, however, a great event of their century—the Depression of the 1930s—thrust Grace and Joe together. Again, they shared their deepest thoughts and emotions.

By that time, Joe had married Grace's sister Olive. They had two children, myself and my brother Joe, Jr. Our father managed the Commercial Bank in Okanogan Valley, a remote ravine running north and south along the east foothills of the Cascade Mountains. Grace had established a thriving interior decorating business in Spokane, seemingly unaffected by hard times. Her first clients were her old painting students, her former schoolmates, and a few wealthy families she had met in childhood during her parents' migration from town to town in Eastern Washington.

My father, now Grace's brother-in-law, was searching for money to keep his bank open. He had tried in Seattle and Portland, without success. Spokane was his last stop to avert at least temporary financial ruin.

Grace would send him off in the morning with a substantial breakfast. They communed again mid-day to discuss strategy and her different perspectives on his financing problems. She steered him to her own Spokane contacts, such as Joe Bailey, a bank president who had helped finance both her mother and herself. In the evenings, she planned his relaxation: a show, an interesting new restaurant, or a scenic walk.

Without flaunting her own well-being, Grace offered to lend Joe all the money he needed to keep his bank open.

"I will not drag anyone else down with me," Joe replied, "especially you."

He was a good businessman, but in aspects of business for which Grace cared little: making money, keeping records, and planning carefully. She was in business to create; he, to provide.

Despite the bank closing, Joe worked his way out of debt, as his father J.D. had before. The personal price was high. He developed bleeding stomach ulcers and, months before operations were abandoned for such ailments, had major surgery. He died at the age of 50 in 1938.

From the 1930s through the 1960s, Grace's friendship with Raymond Enloe deepened. Raymond's father, Eugene Enloe, had foreseen more acutely than J.D. Bassett, the Columbia River not as a transportation route but as a power source, primarily for electricity. "Papa" Enloe's life reads like an Horatio Alger success story. From a beginning in Medical Lake as a baker, banker, and close friend of the Joneses, he rose to head numerous Northwest businesses, including power companies which eventually merged with the great Washington Water Power Company. His son, Raymond, ran local electrical offices in Alberta and in Okanogan, Washington, where he met and married his wife Helen. Later, he was president of the Idaho Portland Cement Company and served on the Board of Directors of half a dozen major corporations including Washington Water Power, Hotel Spokane, and the Washington Trust Bank.

From their 40s through 60s, Raymond and Helen, probably Grace's closest friends, often played and worked together, usually in and around the Enloe home for which Grace was the primary decorator. Once Raymond and Grace spent a day on their hands and knees, placing and replacing stones Helen had envisioned as a unique walkway to the garden. The stone workers, both personages in the city, obligingly promised to create a whole new garden if they could abandon her criss-cross pattern. Laughing at their misplacements of the stones, soiled knees and all, they retired to a good wine and splendid dinner together. It was a typical day for Grace with the Enloes, who, childless, made Grace part of their family.

David Gaiser, a minister's son, who as a child had toddled after the teenage Grace, became a doctor and continued to serve her as her personal physician and friend through Grace's midyears. She decorated the Gaiser home, too, presided over by another childhood friend, Helen Broughton. After Helen's death, Dr. Gaiser married Mary Jewett, a principal benefactor of a myriad of Northwest institutions and charities.

Both the Enloes and Gaisers lived in a kind of comfort that was meaningless to Grace herself. She kept her living quarters spare, saving her special arrangements and centers of interest to be adapted for other homes and other lives.

Grace dismissed, with the wave of her hand, another man, a rumored Danish count she met while she was in Europe. He accompanied her to the Flemish country and showed her the studios of several European painters. Grace's sister insisted he pursued her as a potential wife. Grace's wave of the hand neither confirmed nor denied.

Despite the many men in her life, Grace never married for at least three reasons. First, during her 20s, most American men were fighting World War I in Europe. Second, she believed she could contribute more through art than through family. Third, an awful experience in her early 30s created a doubt in her mind that she could safely raise children.

She was haunted forever after the day she was stopped in her car by a red light. The light changed. She started across the intersection. Suddenly, a little girl ran into the path of her car. The youngster had broken from the grasp of two older children and, out of the line of Grace's vision, darted into the street. The child was dead. Grace had killed her. A court was to clear Grace of any responsibility.

Grace never spoke to me of that devastating accident. Her sister, my mother, told me about it. Afterward, whenever she could, Grace relied on others to drive her. She was equally nervous in a car whether she or someone else was driving. At the lake, she was terrified that a child might fall over the cliffs on her property.

Sometimes she said that little children, no matter how loved or protected, always were in danger of serious injury, a life-long handicap, or death.

If she could have overcome her fears of nurturing children and found a way, in her era, to dedicate herself to both career and family, she well might have chosen a husband from the men in her life.

CHAPTER FOUR

The Professional Woman

FIRST CREATIONS

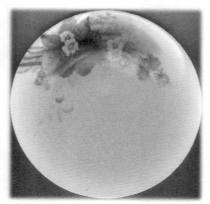

ONE OF GRACE'S HAND-PAINTED
CHINA PLATES

RESTORATION OF CAMPBELL HOUSE

The Professional Woman

"I have one talent. My talent is color."

Thus, Grace reflected on her 55-year career in interior decorating.

Just as deep and mysterious as her eye for color was another talent that assured her success in business. She could see into people. She could detect what many never see: intent, flexibility, energy, and the degree to which a mind is opened or closed. This insight was the basis of her relationships with clients. So she began by knowing her customer. Then she worked within the bounds of her customer's interests and capacities.

As those capacities expanded, so did the imagination and taste. Grace became almost flawless in making these initial assessments, and they often led to life-long associations or, on the other hand, to a quick but extremely courteous decision not to take a customer. After their first conversation, I have heard Grace tell a would-be client how sorry she was: she had checked her work schedule and she would be unable to meet the client's time needs. If the client—whether woman or man—

persisted, Grace's closing line might be: "I am deeply sorry but I have analyzed your situation and mine carefully, and I am quite certain you will be more satisfied with the services of another decorator, given our respective situations."

And she was sorry. But her decision to work or not to work with someone was the first step in a process that created beauty for many people.

When she accepted a client, the go-ahead was usually because Grace sensed an openness, a potential for growth, and a passion to learn and to experience. The cut-off almost always stemmed from the prospect's certainty that she knew exactly what she wanted Grace to do for her. This, for Grace, signaled a diminution of mutual creativity. Mutuality being her goal, she never started on what couldn't work.

It was this ability to know what made creative ideas work that distinguished her. Like her father, in a sense, Grace ministered to her clients. More like her mother, she made clear-cut judgements based on her sensitivity to human nature. She became so accurate in these assessments that her success was virtually assured when she began working with a family.

She cut to the truth, through detail to substance, in her private, as well as professional, dealings. She also maintained her faith in a grand design that implied God—never presuming, however, to impose her standards on others.

Drawn to those gifts, young and old tended to confide in her on matters other than decorating problems. One woman, in love with a married man with two children, sought Grace's advice. But no moral judgement, no recriminations came from

Grace. Her response: "Remember, he has felt before all that you are now feeling for the first time."

A charming but distraught 25-year-old bachelor told Grace that his wedding date had been set in three weeks because he had gotten a girl pregnant and, in the meantime, he had been fighting nightly with the priest giving him instructions for joining the church of his bride-to-be.

Grace called him back to her house the next day with her own instructions: Call a doctor, whose name and telephone number she provided; call him from her phone; arrange for a test; set up an appointment that afternoon for the girl; and escort her to the doctor's office.

The wedding was called off. The girl was not pregnant after all.

A 12-year-old youngster confided to Grace that she wanted to be an interior decorator when she grew up, but she did not know how to begin. "You can test yourself," Grace assured her. "Find a color in your room. Look at it carefully. Then go to a fabric shop or a department store, a hardware or paint store— somewhere with color samples. Find your color and take home the sample to see if it matches."

The little girl, now in her 70s, said that she did that, adding: "I still do it."

One matron used Grace for such diverse services as re-decorating for grand entertaining in her home and even for arranging chocolates on her Tiffany tray.

Color expressed human characteristics for Grace. She described the energy of one of Spokane's first woman doctors by saying, "Her black eyes shine." Asked the mood of another friend, prone to depression, Grace said: "Purple emerging to blue."

She resumed china-painting classes, this time at Spokane University, which existed from 1913 to 1933. Her moniker in the university annual was "Grace Jones, Director of China Painting and Interior Decoration."

In these first decades of the 20th Century, more women edged into the marketplace by painting china than by any other avenue. In fact, until the Second World War never before had so many American women produced products for sale as did those thousands of amateurs who, like Grace's students, designed and painted china. Only Rosie the Riveter and her millions of compatriots, who took the places of men fighting overseas in the 1940s, surpassed these pioneer china painters as a feminine presence in the American economy.

Grace's business, initially for reasons of income, was at first partially a gift shop. A burst of Christmas buying soon identified her studio on the north side of Second and Howard in Spokane to a much larger circle than her former school and china-painting friends.

She worked and lived for the last 45 years of her life at subsequent studios on the south side of Fourth and Howard and at 409 West Fifth Avenue. Both these properties soon will be incorporated into the campus of Lewis and Clark High School.

Grace lived upstairs from her studio, with almost complete disregard for her own comfort. Her rooms were Spartan in

GRACE'S STUDIO-HOME

their simplicity. None of the care and personal attention she lavished on her clients was evident. She seldom cooked and viewed housekeeping as a waste of time. Real life, for her, was in her friendships and downstairs in her studio.

The studio consisted of a showroom, a workroom, and a storage room, plus kitchen, bath, and basement shop for furniture repair and finishing. Pictures—originals and prints— were stored in a large cabinet. A glass display case featured smaller items.

Her staff numbered between four and five; always Clarence Heineman, her faithful assistant; at least three seamstresses; and usually an assistant decorator.

Three seamstresses were at sewing machines in the workroom beyond. They were "Hummer," the director; "Sadisk"; and "Kathy." A giant cutting table stood along the length of the room. Here, Grace and her women measured and cut material for curtains, bedspreads, pillowcovers, and upholstery. Two built-in cupboards contained sewing accessories. On the far side of the worktable were wall-to-wall shelves of fabric samples. In the storage room were higher, longer shelves containing rolls of fabric.

She had that knack, so rare among employers, of communicating her respect and admiration for her employees' talents. "Exquisitely stitched" or "You are a seamstress of rare talent," she would tell her workers. Clarence, her jack-of-all-trades from age 18 to 83, knew he was irreplaceable.

One young man, Bill Farrington, sought Grace's advice about how to become an interior designer. After several talks, her opinion was: "He has everything he needs to be successful except an education." So Grace educated him by hiring him for several years. And when they both felt he was ready, she helped him launch his own business—which was, so long as Bill lived, her major competition.

BILL FARRINGTON

In this setting, for more than half a century, she followed a daily schedule that would have exhausted anyone years younger. For decades, her small body required little more than four hours sleep. The days generally were divided into four main parts: work in the studio, pre-dawn to noon; luncheon meetings and house calls, noon to 5 p.m.; closing the workroom and socializing with friends from five o'clock until well into the evening; and finally, bookkeeping to midnight. For at least an hour between midnight and her pre-dawn rising hour, she was in bed reading books, magazine articles, and the day's newspaper.

She danced downstairs to her studio about 6 a.m., with a bright, "Good morning, morning" or "Good morning" to anything else she happened to see, such as "dog," "sun," "fog," or, if he had arrived, her faithful "Clarence."

Preparations for the day began immediately. She had two hours before her seamstresses arrived. She assembled samples of materials for different decorating projects underway. Bright sunlight streamed through a giant window facing east. More muted light came from other windows. She tested the blend of fabric colors in each light. If there were fabrics to be cut, she and Clarence laid them out on the big worktable, edged with measuring sticks, and topped with thick fabric. By the time Hummer, Sadisk, and Kathy walked in, their assignments lay outlined on each sewing machine. Clarence and Grace helped them get started.

Then, depending on the day, there were phone calls, more sample and fabric assemblages, as well as deliveries and other chores away from the studio, almost all done by Clarence. By noon, Grace was ready for consultations and home visits with clients, her fabrics in the station wagon and any furniture pieces strapped on top.

At the end of the afternoon, Grace and her seamstresses inspected the day's work, examined problems, and found solutions before the women went home, usually praised by Grace and satisfied with their production.

The scope of her work stretched from World War II recreational centers in the Philippines, Hawaii, and a four-state area—Washington, Idaho, Montana, and Oregon—to the East Coast. She frequently was on the road to state universities in those states to decorate fraternity and sorority houses. In Pullman, Washington, site of Washington State University, Grace noted that a burgeoning intellectual society had no bookstore. So she established one. She hired a resident manager and set up a system of sales, rentals, and loans of books and magazines. Through the 1940s and 1950s, the store supplied the college town with music and art treatises as well.

Resorts called on her, too, including Chet Huntley's ranch in Montana. And numerous lakefront property owners asked for her help. A judge and his wife gleefully remembered hoisting tiny Grace by her elbows and hands, and carrying her, suspended over knee-deep snow, as they stumbled down the road to their cabin.

SHEPHERDING EIGHT GUESTS THROUGH SIX FEET OF SNOW ON A 20-DEGREES-BELOW-ZERO NEW YEAR'S EVE—THAT WAS GRACE'S IDEA OF A PARTY. THIS PASTE-UP WAS GUEST HAROLD BOYD'S THANK-YOU NOTE.

The style and feeling of the interiors she designed were as diverse as her friends and clients. Their names are best known today by the names on business buildings in downtown Spokane and on letterheads of local law firms, foundations, and corporations, such names as: Bailey, Barnes, Barnett, Barrett, Beard, Boyd, Brewer, Broughton, Calkins, Clark, Coon, Cowles, Davenport, Farmin, Fix, Foley, Gaiser, Graham, Hartson, Hawkins, Hazen, Heylman, Higgins, Marshall, Martin, McCallister, Paulsen, Payne, Peyton, Richardson, Salt, Shields, Snoddy, Stanton, Thompson, Weed, and Witherspoon . . . the names go on.

Behind the desk of the senior partner in a leading downtown law firm, Grace devised a back-hinged panel, opening at the touch of a hand into full living quarters for him and his wife—a home away from home. She decorated a penthouse atop one of Spokane's highest buildings, along with its open-air terraces.

She decorated for a man and his wife in a posh South Hill neighborhood, and for his mistress on the north side of town. "Isn't that difficult?" I asked her. "Oh, no. They both love blue."

One of her client friends was the Bishop of the Catholic Diocese for Spokane. He called Grace to handle interior and exterior preparations for a large three-day gathering of Catholics from a four-state area. Grace remembered midway through the celebration that some potted plants needed water. She went to the empty cathedral, found a pitcher and water, and was hard at work when the Bishop appeared.

Walking quickly to Grace, he said, "But, Miss Jones, you're watering the plants with the holy water!"

Grace shrugged. "I can't help it, Father. I don't belong to your Lodge." The plants blossomed as did the friendship between Grace and the Bishop.

A couple who ran a nightclub asked Grace to decorate a six-bedroom house, where their employees could rest and enjoy privacy after hours. "The girls need a quiet place after their hectic nights," the owners explained.

Grace inquired whether all bedrooms should be restful or some exciting.

"Use your own judgement," they replied.

As usual, Grace did. And the owners could not have been more pleased with her finished product.

If her open-mindedness occasionally caused awkwardness, Grace could restore harmony with a quip. In 1966, when she was 75, I was in Spokane for a quick visit. She dragged me to a formal dinner for ten. The table conversation turned to Vietnam. The other guests considered the conflict a footnote in history, soon to be settled in our favor, a cold war victory stemming the Red Tide in Asia.

Back East, I was involved in anti-war protests and planning a presidential campaign for Eugene McCarthy. Grace's glance reminded me to keep silent. But soon, as a newspaperwoman covering Lyndon Johnson's White House, I was being importuned for my views. Truth was the only way out. I said I thought our action smacked more of colonialism in the French style than anti-communism, that the Administration was deceiving Congress about the human and dollar costs, that we were promising more than the Vietnamese wanted, and that they would suffer terribly because of us. These may have become common-place views at the turn of the 21st century, but they were more startling in Spokane in the mid-1960s. The silence was deafening. Expressions turned to disbelief, disgust, and even anger.

Grace suddenly broke the silence. "Don't pay any attention to her," she said, with a flick of her wrist. "She's a Communist."

The talk returned to pleasant familiarities.

You may be sure that that evening Grace and I discussed Vietnam at length. We fell asleep speculating how Communists would repel or attract Hindus, Buddhists, Shintoists, and followers of Confucius.

Once a man was showing Grace through his home. She noticed a decorative stove in a corner of a small room.

"Why did you put the stove there?" she asked.

"Because there was a hole in the ceiling," he replied, pointing.

"Ah," Grace said. "Monkey see, monkey do."

Her host reached into a fruit bowl and turned back to his friend Grace, eating a banana.

Even in old age, Grace was still growing. In terms of training and experience and tenure, she was the leading interior designer in the Northwest. Her reputation persisted. And she was about to engage in the last passion of her life, the restoration of the turn-of-the-20th-century mansion on a bluff overlooking the Spokane River.

She had been thinking more and more about the forces that had shaped Spokane, the relatively remote city she had adopted in her teens. During her early years, its history had been made by adventurers who amassed great fortunes by discovering silver and gold and farming vast lands made available by the Homestead Act of the 19th Century.

The fortunate few who found silver or gold and harvested huge crops of wheat built mansions along the banks of the Spokane River. They spent as much as they made—on their homes, grounds, and families. Their influence set the tone of Spokane to the 21st Century and beyond. Spokanites, by and large, lived for their families. They adapted their attitudes and habits to powerful forces of nature—the water, the mountains, the change of seasons.

Grace marveled at how these attitudes and habits strengthened through the years, and she saw as a symbol of this way of life the great mansion built in 1898 by "Mace" Campbell, one of the lucky ones who had made millions by staking claims near producing silver mines and buying stock in the companies that owned them.

Mace and his wife hired prominent architects and decorators to make real their dream home, an L-shaped structure on the rim of a bluff high above the river, with verandas, fountains, stables, and a gazebo facing the sunset.

By the 1920s, the elder Campbells were dead. Their daughter, Helen Powell, sold, auctioned, or gave away the house's interior furnishings to clear it for the use of the State Historical Museum next door. The museum's directors had a covered walkway built, connecting the Campbell House and the museum. Through this link began destruction of the integrity of the mansion. Officials tore out walls on the fourth floor to make room for museum displays, and the first artifacts were moved in.

But progress was slow. People in the 1930s were working their way out of the Great Depression. In the 40s, they were fighting World War II. And in the 50s, they were recuperating from the previous two decades. Only by the 1960s did Grace and a handful of others, fascinated by history, recognize that the Campbell House was a symbol of Northwest history. Never before or after had families in Spokane lived at the pace or economic level of those early adventurers who had struck it rich.

Why not preserve such a symbol of those lush times—by re-creating authentically the setting in which the Campbells had lived?

The problem was that the Campbell House was now a state historical museum, filled with rocks, displaying the geological history of the Northwest. Walls were torn out on the third floor. Scheduled to be moved in were relics both of the native Indian tribes and of the settlers from the East.

Grace analyzed the problem and resolved it systematically. She saw two major priorities: to form a committee to raise funds for the restoration, semi-independent of the museum board; and to assure the authenticity of the restoration.

And she set three goals: to get back the original furnishings from the buyers, friends, and descendants who now owned them; to overcome the opposition of those who preferred a beautiful restoration over an authentic one; and to search the house and grounds for remains of original installations and replicate them exactly.

She started with the kitchen. The Paulsens, one of Spokane's first families, donated a huge black-and-silver stove of the period. Grace and her co-workers re-created the cupboards and pantries, storage areas, and worktables that the family's servants would have used in the early 1900s.

"The kitchen first," she said. "Then they cannot move rocks in here." "Rocks" came to be her abbreviation (no prejudice involved) for general museum exhibits.

Up went a replica of the original wall covering in the great side hall and stairwell. Grace had it fabricated in Japan by a firm she had come to know through buying trips. The design was bold, verging on the gaudy to some critics. Gigantic red poppies burst from long, multicolored green stems. Grace caught the green-and-rosy-red motif in decorations throughout the house.

The Campbells had welcomed their guests in a glittering gilt parlor to the right of the entrance. To the left, a large living room featured clusters of comfortable chairs and a central table where both adults and children worked, read, and played games. Up a few steps was the dining room with a Delft-tile fireplace; its blue and white set the tone for this room, from which the family could go out onto the enormous terrace overlooking the river. The Campbells and their only child, their daughter Helen, slept in bedrooms on the second floor, with

THE CAMPBELL HOUSE, 1998

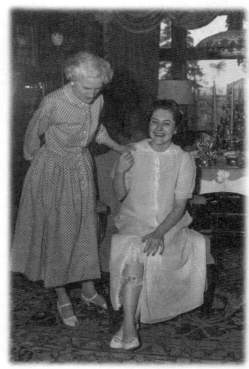

GRACE, AT A CAMPBELL HOUSE
FUNDRAISER, WITH MAJOR BENEFACTOR
HELEN PAULSEN, SPOKANE

CAMPBELL HOUSE DINING ROOM

mammoth marble-and-mahogany bathrooms adjoining. The Campbell servants had more living space than the family: a separate dining room with a stairway leading to their fourth floor quarters and a half-dozen bedrooms.

Grace sensed a coolness toward the project in the Campbells' daughter, Helen Powell, who perhaps had an idealized memory of the house of her youth rather than a literal one. To close the distance between Mrs. Powell and the restoration committee, Grace persuaded her close friend, Helen Enloe, who was also a close friend of Helen Powell, to serve with the group. So the conduit was established. The Campbell daughter's feelings were respected; the committee's search for authenticity was respected; and communication was clear, if not direct.

In 1980, with the kitchen rebuilt, the reception and dining rooms restored, the downstairs den rejuvenated, Grace, aged

89, resigned as chair of the committee. She acknowledged in her letter of resignation, which she set before her committee members, "It is time for new leadership."

She had helped assure the authentic restoration of all four floors of the Campbell House. Financing was beginning to flow in from the state and other public sources. The house was physically separated from the museum. And shortly after Grace's death in 1981, an enlightened museum management recognized that the dual entities—mansion and museum—deserved equal attention.

Restoration, post Grace Jones, has become more expert, better financed. The project's directors worked from a sound base. They built on those first invaluable contributions of Grace's committee. One of her confidants among that group, Helen Enloe, went so far as to say:

"But for Grace Jones, there never would have been a restored Campbell House."

THE CAMPBELL HOUSE

CHAPTER FIVE

The Last of Life

HAWAII

ELEUTHERA ISLAND, BAHAMAS

NEWMAN LAKE

GRACE, WITH THE AUTHOR AND HER DOG ROBIN, AT CHESAPEAKE BAY

The Last of Life

G race conducted her business until she was 86. The seamstresses, Kathy, Sadisk, and finally Hummer, were let go. Her loyal assistant, Clarence, had died three years earlier.

Grace's eyes, the fulcrum of her professional balance, began to fail. No longer could she read those books, letters, or magazines at night. She began to feel a successor could better serve her beloved Campbell House and she resigned as chairman of its restoration committee.

She continued to reach out to people, especially younger generations. Rousing herself, at 88, from in-bed daycare, for example, she attended a wedding of the youngest generation of a family close to her. She attended matches of her favorite sport, hockey. She lunched or dined with friends. The latter were carefully chosen because Grace was eating ever more slowly. A doctor told her mistakenly that she had an ingrown goiter.

Generous to a fault, she explained to a young friend to whom she had promised to lend her car for a sojourn in Seattle:

"Let me explain why I've decided to renege on my promise. You reach a point in your life when the only new things are what you lose. And if there is anything you can do to keep from losing anything else, you do it."

Grace made an unusual move to compensate for one loss— the death of her sister Olive, my mother, in 1968.

Several months afterward, she called me in Washington, D.C., and asked, "Has it occurred to you that we both are motherless?"

Anticipating advice on how to cope with the loss of parents, I told her I could learn from her having lived that experience for more than half a century.

Then came another question: "How would you like to have a mother?"

"I would love to have a mother, but only if it is you."

"Very well," Grace concluded. "I shall put the papers in the mail today." She hung up.

When the adoption papers arrived, I took them to the Captain of the Guards at the U.S. Senate office building, where I was covering a hearing for my newspaper. The Captain was delighted to notarize Grace's becoming a mother at age 78. We celebrated together the next Mother's Day. And I had a generous, thoughtful, lively, and loving mother for another 12 years.

The mechanics of her life continued to be well organized. Her bookkeeper came to her house once a month. As they conferred, her mail got answered and her tax records kept. Housecleaners did their pre-arranged chores.

One of the losses of these years was her right to drive legally. Yet she continued to travel with younger drivers.

Insisting at age 87 on attending my graduation from Georgetown University Law School, Grace flew to Washington, D.C., with a friend, explaining to me:

"I do not believe you did this. I have to see it."

THE AUTHOR AT HER LAW SCHOOL GRADUATION
WITH GRACE, 1979

Her lake place delighted her still.

"This is not the most beautiful place in the world," she said at 89, seated on one of the giant flat rocks of Council Bluff and looking toward the path to the beach. "But there is no other place just like it, is there?"

A few years earlier, noting her physical weaknesses, I had sold my home in Georgetown and bought a larger duplex off Connecticut Avenue and 18th Street in Washington, partly because many lawyers have offices on 18th Street. The duplex had a separate apartment at street level, if Grace should ever need it. When Grace toured the place, she asked me why I had bought the house. I mentioned it was near the center of law practices and provided a possible office for me or guest quarters or a rental unit.

As usual, Grace saw to the truth. She looked me in the eye, came close to me, and wiggled her finger an inch from my nose. "If I am blind and paralyzed," she said, pausing for emphasis, "don't you dare move me to Washington, D.C."

The message was clear. And it set me to ruminating about Grace's full life: the play of a Victorian upbringing by her duty-driven father and sensitive mother, both immigrants to this country; their frequent moves during her childhood, forcing her, before age 15, to start over again many times in different towns, different schools; and her discovery, with her mother's help that winter in Southern California, of the first clues to how she must live independently and creatively. She chose as a symbol of her own personal identity the Spanish name "Consuela." This was Consuela speaking. She had put down her roots in Spokane, Washington. And that was where she intended to stay, especially as she approached death.

Throughout her mature life, she had responded to her childhood influences by growing in four fascinating ways I could identify.

First, she settled on stern moral values for herself and total tolerance for different ways of life. Indeed, she welcomed differences among people and delighted in exploring them.

Second, and perhaps more fundamental to her character, she answered an inner call to live creatively. Forsaking the intimacy of family life, she found self-fulfillment in sharing and shaping beauty in the lives of others.

Third, apart from her well-prepared and executed professional life, she took time every day to be a friend. She always put aside professional demands to build trust or broaden personal understanding.

Finally, she lent every experience a unique energetic joy.

As she aged, her view of doctors grew bemused. Twice, they had pronounced her dead. The first time was at the Campbell House. She fainted while attending a large fundraiser. There was a doctor in the house. "I'm sorry. She is dead," he said, after kneeling to attend her.

"Grace wouldn't die on me," a friend protested. Other concerned friends hovered. An ambulance had been called when Grace sat up and inquired what she was doing on the floor. Her friend lifted her into a chair, and within 30 minutes, Grace seemed as sprightly as ever.

The second time was in the hospital before the operation that would prove fatal. She was sitting up rigidly in her bed when I visited her before breakfast. I raced to the nurses' desk: "Grace is not responding!"

Buzzers. Bells. Nurses, a doctor, and a minister appeared in seconds. The doctor, a young man with an angelic face, leaned over Grace, shook his head, and said, "No sign of life." There were claps, shakes, a little pounding.

Grace opened her eyes. Reaching her right hand to the doctor's cheek, she asked, "Are you God?"

As a consequence of these two events, Grace made only one last request of me: "Make sure I'm dead."

Doctors told me earlier when I was first ushered to her hospital bedside, "She does not understand what is said. That is why we have been unable to gain her permission for an operation."

At her bedside, Grace motioned me close. "The doctors here believe I do not have good sense. I understand. They are young. I am old. But I do have good sense. And I want you to remember as we review our options that the operation they recommend has different meanings for us. To them, it is a very interesting operation. To me, it is my life."

The decision to operate was made after Grace called in a doctor friend, who was unaffiliated with the hospital. He explained fully what had not been communicated at all to her before. Her "ingrown goiter" had been misdiagnosed for 16 years. She suffered from a diverticulum of the esophagus; the pouch was as big as a lung.

"Very well," Grace said. "Let's operate as soon as possible."

The lightness of her spirit prevailed, even through this final ordeal. When a friend asked what she could do for her, Grace replied: "You may restore my health. Then give me a tin cup filled with gold coins to pay for it."

Three excruciatingly painful days later, Grace was dead.

Her memorial service was at the Campbell House. A friend, Margy (Mrs. Philip) Stanton, organized it beautifully, despite initial protests that the Campbell House was not established for funerals.

"The Campbell House is Grace Jones' home," Mrs. Stanton said, and all agreed.

Before the memorial, Grace's body was buried near that of her father and mother. The plot, as she requested, was open grass between two trees. The only marker is a large, bench-shaped boulder. We sit there, remembering what we can know of Grace, in a place more like a park than a cemetery.

The memory resounding for me—beyond her death, memorial, and burial—was of our last evening together at the lake. We were sitting on the terrace, sipping a drink, and watching the sunset. It was her favorite time.

Out of the quiet, the color, and the beauty, she said: "I do not mind dying. I am not afraid to die. My only regret is there may be no sunsets in heaven."

EPILOGUE

VISITING AUNT GRACE
by
Laurie Porter Combs †

Crystal water
sparkling with light
I water skied there, skimming
the glistening surface
of cool darkness
riding the sky
flying
for my very first time
Pine woods
sun trickling through, touching
layer upon layer of pine needle floors

It is she I remember
tall and graying
stately

or perhaps my faded
memories are not
her, but only glimpses
of myself, in an old
dead woman?

An old
woman, slim and gracious
like my father's mother
Grammy
who died when I was five
now Aunt Grace has
died

do those here always
see the faces
of their dead
in the living?

Aunt Grace drove us out to the lake
where a cabin in the woods
invited us in
the back door and out
the front door through scraggly
blueberries and wild
grasses sparsely
covering gray lichened rocks
down to the water
Lichen spotted pines
grew firmly
from cracks in the rock, never
letting go, not even long
after they were dead

Perhaps she is now
speaking with Grammy, perhaps
it was my father who met her, so
glad to see her
asking why
didn't she come in for a while
            I want to see my father
            and Grammy
            and Aunt Grace

            Maybe they aren't really gone

Aunt Grace was a pine
            She found tiny cracks
            set her roots way
            down as far
            as she could and grew

and grew and made those cracks wider
and longer

She was a rock cracker
                    Lots happened
                    Grasses put their little feet down
                    super-glued them there
                    Some dirt bugs came
                    a spider
                    and a squirrel, every
                    day to sit at the foot
                    of Aunt Grace and crack
                    nuts in the sun
                    on the rock
                    by the crack
Other trees came
                    they watched Aunt Grace
                    they started cracking rocks too

                    Grammy was a rock cracker
                    so was my Dad

        The lake was quiet
        and still
        at dusk, except
        for the drone of a distant
        motor boat that also quieted
        as dark descended more heavily
        The lights across the way
        one by one
        ignited, defining the dark mass
        of the other shore

---

† The poet, at 19, wrote this recollection of her visit, at 10, to Grace at Newman
    Lake. Laurie Porter was a student at the University of Michigan which awarded
    her the annual Hopwood Prize for Literature.

"Beauty is truth, truth beauty,"—that is all
Ye know on earth, and all ye need to know.

—*John Keats*

ABOUT THE AUTHOR

M. G. Bassett, journalist and lawyer, wrote for *The Washington Post*, *The Washington Star*, and King Features Syndicate in Washington, D.C., from 1952 to 1976, with frequent breaks for study and travel.

Covering Congress, the White House, and political campaigns, she also served as Assistant Cabinet Secretary for Republican President Gerald Ford and as Assistant Campaign Manager for Democratic Presidential Candidate Eugene McCarthy.

The author won a number of newspaper awards, had a one-on-one radio interview program, and often appeared on television news panels. Her work also includes studies for foundations and institutes. She was graduated from Whitman College, the Columbia University Pulitzer School of Journalism, the Georgetown University Law Center, and attended the University of Michigan Law School. In Europe, she studied at the University of Paris and the University of Frankfurt. She was born in Spokane; grew up in Okanogan, Washington; was the granddaughter of Grace's British parents; and on the Bassett side, descended from early comers to New England.

PHOTO BY JEREMY NICKELSON
DAYTON, WASHINGTON

THE AUTHOR BESIDE STAINED GLASS GRACE'S FATHER PUT
IN A CHURCH IN DAYTON, WASHINGTON.